MILTON ON MY MIND

MILTON ON MY MIND

Essays And Poems

IDA FASEL

REFLECTIONS ON
PARADISE LOST
By
JOHN MILTON

authorHOUSE®

AuthorHouse™
1663 Liberty Drive
Bloomington, IN 47403
www.authorhouse.com
Phone: 1-800-839-8640

First published by AuthorHouse   05/20/2011

ISBN: 978-1-4634-1049-0 (sc)
ISBN: 978-1-4634-1048-3 (dj)
ISBN: 978-1-4634-1047-6 (ebk)

Library of Congress Control Number: 2011908629

Printed in the United States of America

MILTON ON MY MIND

CONTENTS

I: INTRODUCTION

II: ANTHOLOGY EXCERPTS

III: COMMENTARIES AND ESSAYS

IV: MILTON ON MY MIND: A TRIBUTE

ACKNOWLEDGMENTS

How can I thank all those whose interest at my poetry readings spurred me to a simple, thoughtful interpretation of *Paradise Lost* that made meaning the most important ingredient, not the learning. Milton was a musician and a poet. To have read him aloud was the best beginning. I remember the warmth of those faces; the names have slipped away, but their support is one of the memorable lasting things, and I am grateful for their willingness to see Milton as a real human being.

As for friends with names, my only regret is that some will be left out. However, I especially want to thank Sally Kurtzman, Vickie Wilson, Alyssa Kapnik, and Anita Jepson-Gilbert, who did so much to put this manuscript into a presentable state for publication.

CREDITS

The following poems from this volume previously appeared in other publications:

"Adam Naming the Animals," *Where is the Center of the World*, Ida Fasel, 1998.

"A Gratitude for My Husband's Hand," *Bellowing Ark*, Sept./Oct. 2008.

"Creators," *Leafy as a Locust Tree*, 2005.

"Cracking Open a Geode," *Cotyledon*, 2004

"Out of Nothing," *Bellowing Ark*, Sept./Oct. 2008.

"Patterns," *The Deronda Review*, Vol. I, no. 2.

"Rock Hound," *Orbis*, Spring 2003.

"Thoughts on Gustav Davidson's A Dictionary of Angels," *Bellowing Ark*, Sept./Oct. 2008.

"True Freedom I Significant Bondage," *The Difficult Inch*," Ida Fasel, 2000.

"Unequal Exchanges," *Where is the Center of the World*, Ida Fasel, 1998.

"Where the Light Falls," *The Difficult Inch*, Ida Fasel, 2000.

I

INTRODUCTION

DIVINE BEGINNINGS AND BLESSED ENDINGS

Behold, I shall do a new thing: *now it shall spring forth.* Was Milton thinking of Isaiah's words (43:19) when he broke through the heady beginning of his last great poem, *Paradise Lost?*

The poem begins in the classical tradition, the middle of things. The war in heaven is over. Good has triumphed over evil. We shall hear the details in later books. Meanwhile, Satan, with his great horde of rebel angels, is driven from heaven and falls in flames to hell, his new home intended for permanence. Once arrived, he lies plotting against his replacement in God's Love, newly created man, recently established in a newly created second heaven.

From then on, the poem winds though its dramatic story to the major event, the Biblical Fall and its resolution, leaving Adam and Eve at the brink of a new world and a marriage which is stronger for maturity in which it is understood.

God is glorified in song and justified by firmness before human frailty, yet touched by human sweetness. Obedience is the keynote in Milton's religion of heart. In view of the regrettable things people do to themselves and the awful things they do to each other, God's guidance is a blessing.

There is a commonly held notion (by those who have little knowledge of him) that Milton is heavy, Latinate, argumentative, overblown, in short, boring. To me, after years of living with him and teaching him, admiring him, sharing his search for spirit, intellectually and emotionally, he is very much alive, God the very fiber of his being.

It took years of preparation, thought and learning to write the poem that established his greatness, *Paradise Lost.* His eyes steadily weakened in his 40's. Memory and a fine mind worked for him. His scholarship enriches the writing with its depth of reference. Friends helped. A lifetime of feeling and thought gave him the essence of what matters—to be in the constant presence of God, though outwardly engaged in the work of the day. He was about 50—and totally blind—when he felt ready to follow his heart.

I have long wanted to compile an anthology of passages from this incomparable epic to introduce him to the general reader. To my knowledge few, if any selections I have chosen, are to be found in collections of spiritual poems. My contribution is only a sampling of poems within the whole poem, which he called his "Song."

Paradise Lost was published in 1667. A second edition, with a few changes, followed in 1671, a month short of his 66th birthday. Like the Bible, the poem is one of the great works of Western civilization. It is richly and imaginatively developed, with masterly command of poetic technique and a perfect ear for the sense and sound of words.

My introduction is in three parts. The first is my own long delayed selection of his spiritual poems. The second is made up of prose commentaries on the poems, extended by a few related essays. The third contains select and new poems of my own which I offer as a modest tribute.

You will need a copy of the complete poem. One with notes may be helpful. The anthology poems are to be read aloud and often. Reading the rest aloud repays, for meaning emerges with the music. If your acquaintance with the Bible needs refreshing, acquire a good translation.

Walk humbly with the mystery. Climb the ladder to the sublime, each step "mysteriously meant." Milton, poet, musician, metaphysician, in the bright illumination of his blind eyes, sees images of imagined thoughts, hears in the music of the laws the wisdom and beauty of character,

formed to the best and noblest of values, society regulated by pragmatic wisdom and ideal beauty. Harmony is the key word in his spiritual goal of man and God as one, face to face; nature and Paradise, one; cosmos and heaven, one, in music of the spheres; time and eternity, one, for all time in the fullness of faith and the goodness of God. All else is foam.

Milton was born on December 9, 1608. His 400th anniversary was celebrated by Milton admirers the world, over. His is a poetry of the timeless, a pursuit of perfection in imperfect human beings, universal values of character and conduct, writing of integrity and exquisite vision, of spiritual worth. Read him aloud and you will hear him speaking to you. In 2008 the air was filled with quotations. When next he is so honored, perhaps one of the voices may be yours.

II

ANTHOLOGY EXCERPTS

WITH THEE CONVERSING

Eve is speaking:

> With thee conversing I forget all time,
> All seasons and their change, all please alike.
> Sweet is the breath of morn. her rising sweet,
> With charm of earliest Birds; pleasant the Sun
> When first in this delightful Land he spreads
> His orient Beams, on herb, tree, fruit, and flower,
> Glistering with dew; fragrant the fertile earth
> After soft showers; and sweet the coming on
> Of grateful Evening mild, then silent Night
> With this her solemn Bird and this fair Noon,
> And these the Gems of Heaven, her starry train:
> But neither breath of Morn when she ascends
> With charm of earliest Birds, nor rising Sun
> On this delightful Land, nor herb, fruit, flower
> Glistering with dew, nor fragrance after showers,
> Nor grateful Evening mild, nor silent Night
> With this her solemn Bird, nor walk by Moon
> Or glittering, Star-light without thee is sweet.
>
> (IV. 639-656)

On the surface it is a love poem that does not mention the word love. So simple a surface to be so solid in depth of feeling! A reader returns to savor the initial effect. It is not necessary to name the various rhetorical means, which makes complexity speak so eloquently for the emotional experience that rises to the sublime by the very simplicity of the language. The opening lines flow smoothly in their plain positive statement of true affection to "But," which abruptly reverses direction and works its way back by neither/nors, word for word, to the beginning.

Placed in context, the little lyric ripples out to wider realms of the heart. Eve converses with Adam. Adam converses with Eve. Adam converses with God, for God is Paradise and Paradise is everywhere little stones are left to corroborate holy places of meeting. Milton converses with God as he writes of communion, spirit to Spirit, grateful to the Word that gave him words of love at the deepest level of prayer.

WITH AN EAR TO AIR

Eve defers to Adam as her superior in knowledge. As they walk to bed, garden to bower, she reflects on the stars above. Why do they shine all night when "sleep has shut all eyes?" Adam responds with Milton's sensitivity to sound in air made holy by divine office. They do not shine in vain.

> Millions of spiritual Creatures walk the Earth
> Unseen, both when we wake, and when we sleep:
> All these with ceaseless praise his works behold
> Both day and night: how often from the steep
> Of echoing Hill or Thicket have we heard
> Celestial voices on the midnight air,
> Sole, or responsive, each to other's voice,
> Singing thir great Creator: oft in bands
> While they keep watch, or nightly rounding walk.
> With Heav'nly touch of instrumental sounds
> In full harmonic number join'd. Thir songs
> Divide the night. and lift our thoughts to Heaven.
>
> (IV. 677-88)

Paradise Lost is filled with music, instrumental and vocal. Milton's interest in music was extensive. He was an organist and a singer. His words move as in dance, rhythmically, orderly, meaningfully. He reverenced the organ for its power to evoke the sublime, surging or soothing, sending its voice through body, mind, and soul. He calls his multifaceted poem a Song, and on one occasion joins the angel choir in heaven singing. He tells us in advance his lines do not jingle with end-rhyme, often forced, but flow in the natural measured rhythm of the native language, drawing sense and sound from line to line. He gets his wish for an answerable style.

A POEM LONGER THAN IT LOOKS

The high point of Adam's "Divine colloquy" with God is summed up in one line:

Submiss: he rear'd me, and Whom thou sought'st I am.

One line—one long line packed tight, swift, teeming with rapture at the end of a spiritual journey, the timeless intervention in prosodic time, the eternal light filling prosodic space, brought face to face with the very Him!—his presence in real presence; his state, one of illumination.

No one has proved that God does not exist. That he is dear to your heart may be your private wisdom and certainty.

IN THE MIDST OF THINGS
"NO MIDDLE FLIGHT"

Invocation I

A torrent of sound, sparkling water cascading over hidden terraces of rock, a grand sweep of the entire subject matter and its development, the language in continuous movement toward its vaulting purpose: 26 lines teeming with significance, every step guided by a far greater power than his own, every word chosen for its deep resources of final meaning in spirituality. Such is the way Milton begins his dramatic poem, in the manner of the classical writers—action already begun—but out of himself in a new burst of creative adventure.

> Of Man's First Disobedience and the Fruit
> Of that Forbidden Tree, whose mortal taste
> Brought Death into the world, and all our woe,
> With loss of Eden, till one greater Man
> Restore us, and regain the blissful Seat,
> Sing Heav'nly Muse, that on the secret top
> of Oreb or of Sinai didst inspire
> That Shepherd, who first taught the chosen Seed,
> In the Beginning how the Heavens and Earth
> Rose out of Chaos: Or if Sion Hill
> Delight thee more, and Siloa's Brook that flow'd
> Fast by the Oracle of God; I thence
> Invoke thy aid to my advent'rous Song
> That with no middle flight intends to soar
> Above th' Aonian. Mount, while it pursues
> Things unattempted yet in Prose or Rhyme.
> And chiefly Thou O Spirit, that dost prefer
> Before all Temples th' upright heart and pure,

> Instruct me, for Thou know'st; Thou from the first
> Wast present, and with mighty wings outspread
> Dove-like satst brooding on the vast Abyss
> And mad'st it pregnant: What in me is dark
> Illumine, what is low raise and support;
> That to the highth of this great Argument
> I may assert Eternal Providence,
> And justify the ways of God to Men.
>
> (I. 1-26)

The emotion that sends these lines plunging toward period hardly derives from learning, but from spirit manifesting itself in ardent willingness to answer to God for the way one uses his gift of life toward achieving "th' upright heart and pure." The Shepherd Moses is intensely present in the appeal to the Holy Spirit for guidance upward. There is as much rapture in those loving opening lines as in Moses' face as he came down from Mount Sinai. No society can survive or individual thrive without a strong moral code, and flawed as the ideal proves when put into practice, the standards of conduce set in the Mosaic commandments, long a staple of Western civilization, in wisdom and civility unmatched, are still observed in countries fortunate enough to understand their value.

Not only does the glorious opening of *Paradise Lost* match the momentous occasion of its coming into being, but it also suggests the state of Milton's mind at the time of writing his poem, a "Song" throughout and at the same time "this great Argument." He does not falter, nor does he overstep the bounds. "And chiefly Thou O Spirit," he prays. "Instruct me." He invokes the Holy Spirit as a person, conversationally accessible, his prayer at its utmost intensity of metaphysical reach. In one of his rare personal statements he attributes his blindness to "the overshadowing of those heavenly wings . . . which, when occasioned, he [God] is wont to illumine with interior light, more precious and more pure." This is not self-pity or self-aggrandizement, but ceaseless gratitude.

EYES FOR THE PARADISE WITHIN

Invocation III

Hail holy Light, offspring of Heav'n first-born
Or of th' Eternal Coeternal beam
May I express thee unblam'd? since God is Light
And never but in unapproached light
Dwelt from Eternity, dwelt then in thee,
Bright effluence of bright essence increate,
Or hear'st thou rather pure Ethereal stream,
Whose Fountain who shall tell? before the Sun,
Before the Heavens thou wert, and at the voice
Of God, as with a Mantle didst invest
The rising world of waters dark and deep,
Won from the void and formless infinite.
Thee I revisit now with bolder wing,
Escap't the Stygian Pool though long detain'd
In that obscure sojourn, while in my flight
Through utter and through middle darkness borne
With other notes than to th' Orphean Lyre
I sung of Chaos and Eternal Night,
Taught by the Heav'nly Muse to venture down
The dark descent and up to reascend
Though hard and rare: Thee I revisit safe,
And feel thy sovran, vital Lamp but thou
Revisit'st not these eyes, that roll in vain
To find thy piercing ray, and find no dawn;
So thick a drop serene hath quencht thir Orbs,
Or dim suffusion veil'd. Yet not the more
Cease I to wander where the Muses haunt
Clear Spring or shady Grove, or Sunny Hill,

Smit with the love of sacred Song; but chief
Thee Sion and the flow'ry Brooks beneath
That wash thy hallow'd feet, and warbling flow,
Nightly I visit: nor sometimes forget
Those other-two equall'd with me in fate.
So were I equall'd with them in renown,
Blind Thamyris and blind Maeonides,
And Tiresias and Phineus Prophets old.
Then feed on thoughts that volumntary move
Harmonious numbers and the wakeful Bird
Sings darkling, and in shadiest Covert hid,
Tunes his nocturnal Note. Thus with the Year
Seasons return, but not to me returns
Day, or the sweet approach of Ev'n or Morn,
Or sight of vernal bloom, or Summer's Rose,
Or flocks, or herds, or human face divine;
But cloud instead, and ever-during dark
Surrounds me, from the cheerful ways of men
Cut off, and for the Book of knowledge fair
Presented with a Universal blanc
Of Nature's works to me expung'd and ras'd,
And wisdom at one entrance quite shut out.
So much the rather thou Celestial Light
Shine inward, and the mind through all her powers
Irradiate, there plant eyes, all mist from thence
Purge and disperse that I may see and tell
Of things invisible to mortal sight.

(III. 1-56)

It is a beautiful poem, a perfect poem in itself, spiritually, morally, personally. I shall discuss it in connection with the other Invocations. It is a shining light for the Paradise within. It makes the world less sordid, happiness more likely to find, the wonder of life more apparent as we live it creatively, lovingly.

HAIL, WEDDED LOVE

Is Mendelssohn's Wedding March still played at church and home weddings? Does Milton's tribute to "wedded love" still add a literary touch to biblical authority? Or do the busy young, tapping away on their little hand machines, prefer to make their own laws and break them at will?

God performed the first marriage. Eve was so naive she fell in love with her own image mirrored in the water and had to be corrected by God, who was taking her to Adam. Her destined husband, if we read the legends, was tall as the sky. Next to God, he was said to know everything. He was unsmiling. Her first response was to run, but he seized her hand—gently, as she put it, assuring her of his lifetime devotion. She came to see his true beauty though it entailed the Fall.

> Hail, Wedded Love
> Hail, wedded Love, mysterious Law, true source
> Of human offspring, sole propriety
> In Paradise of all things common else.
> By thee adulterous lust was driv'n from men
> Among the bestial herds to range, by thee
> Founded in Reason, Loyal, Just, and Pure,
> Relations dear, and all the Charities
> Of Father, Son, and Brothers first were known.
>
> (IV. 750-757)

With Milton's passion for probity, it is not surprising that he should find "married love" ideally one of the beauties of earth. The romantic has no more substance than a dream. The idealist sets his mind on noblest things and knows them unachievable, but happily persists. "Perpetual Fountain of domestic sweets" no marriage can be, as Milton well knew from his own first experience. But let mind and heart combine with the love God has for us; the realistic fades and the totally convincing early days of marriage emerge. And who is to say maturity has not made the marriage of Adam and Eve a better one after the Fall?

When our time comes and we have only reached the bottom rung of God's ladder of values, we may be surprised at how much merit our record shows. I like to think He will come down from the highest to where we are standing, lowest of the low, and greet us with a blessing.

Love—how much there is to it! "Him first, him last, him midst, and without end" (V. 165).

A BENEDICTION

Nothing can dampen Adam's great good will. Hear his words to Raphael at sundown parting after his long visit:

> Go Heavenly Guest, Ethereal Messenger,
> Sent from whose sovran goodness I adore.
> Gentle to me and affable hath been
> Thy condescension, and shall be honor'd ever
> With grateful Memory: thou to mankind
> Be good and friendly still, and oft return.

(VIII. 647-651)

A GRATITUDE TO GOD FOR CREATION

Song of Creation (in part)

It is the seventh day and all heaven is bursting with music. All its instruments—the harp predominating—are in use. The great angels are in song. A blessing for the whole human race in the work God has made.

> To create
> is greater than created to destroy.
> Who can impair thee, mighty King, or bound
> Thy Empire? easily the proud attempt
> Of Spirits apostate and thir Counsels vain
> Thou hast repell'd. while impiously they thought
> Thee to diminish, and from thee withdraw
> The number of thy worshippers. Who seeks
> To lessen thee, against his purpose serves
> To manifest the more thy might: his evil
> Thou usest, and from these creat'st more good.
> Witness the new-made World, another Heaven
> From Heaven Gate not far, founded in view
> On the clear Hyaline, the Glassy Sea;
> Of amplitude almost immense, with Stars
> Numerous, and every Star perhaps a World
> Of destin'd habitation; but thou know'st
> Thir seasons: among these the seat of men,
> Earth with her nether Ocean—circumfus'd
> Thir pleasant dwelling place. Thrice happy men
> And sons of men, whom God had thus advanc't

Created in his Image, there to dwell
And worship him, and in reward to rule
Over his Works, on Earth, in Sea, or Air,
And multiply a Race of Worshippers
Holy and just: thrice happy if they know
Thir happiness, and persevere upright.

(VII. 606-ff.)

LEAVING EDEN

Adam grieves most leaving places where he talked to God.

> This most afflicts me, that departing hence
> As from his face I shall be hid, depriv'd
> His blessed count'nance; here I could frequent,
> With worship, place by place, where he vouchsaf'd
> Presence Divine, and to my Sons relate;
> On this mount he appear'd, under this Tree
> Stood visible, among these Pines his voice
> I heard, here with him at this Fountain talk'd:
> So many grateful Altars would I rear
> Of grassy Turf, and pile up every Stone
> Of lustre from the brook, in memory,
> Or monument of Ages, and thereon
> Offer sweet smelling Gums and Fruits and Flow'rs:
> In yonder nether World where shall I seek
> His bright appearance, or footstep trace?

(XI. 316-329)

The archangel Michael reassures him with these lovely lines, my favorite passage.

> . . . Doubt not but in Valley and in Plain
> God is as here, and will be found alike
> Present, and of his presence many a sign
> Following thee, still compassing thee round
> With goodness and paternal Love, his Face.
> Express, and of his steps the track Divine.

(XI. 349-354)

Places are made sacred by those who bring the sacred to them, Milton tells us. Presumably the stones Adam left to commemorate his encounters with God are still to be found in the rubble of destroyed Paradise. They are the radiant ones.

A LESSON ON LEAVING

Adam, "Greatly in peace of thought," expresses his gratitude to Michael the Archangel on the momentous day of their departure:

> Henceforth I learn, that to obey is best,
> And love with fear the only God, to walk
> As in his presence, ever to observe
> His providence, and on him sole depend,
> Merciful over all his works, with good
> Still overcoming evil, and by small
> Accomplishing great things, by things deem'd weak
> Subverting worldly strong, and worldly wise
> By simply meek; that suffering for Truth's sake
> Is fortitude to highest victory,
> And to the faithful Death the Gate of Life.
>
> (XII. 560-571)

From "celestial Colloquy sublime" to easy, conversational tone, "Till time stand still," till then, how much there is to discuss with God on living well, if we are to live at all.

III

COMMENTARIES and ESSAYS

ABOUT THE VERSE

In the second edition of *Paradise Lost*, Milton explains why he chose not to rhyme his verse in the current fashion. He undertook a prosody of the flowing line in which the sense is drawn out from one line to the next—like conversation but within the metrical bounds of the traditional 10-syllable lines composed of five iambic feet with variations when necessary. It is no more mysterious than the English language itself, which falls naturally into the rhythm we live by and know by ear. Despite expert attempts to make it what it is not, it remains the verse form Adam and Eve used in their morning prayers (V. 149). What a tradition!

I should like to have heard Milton dictating in the early morning hours to his amanuensis. A pity we don't have a recording. Aubrey says he had a light tuneful voice. No doubt he dramatized the powerful passages. He sang. He played the organ. When he came back from Italy, he brought the latest music with him, shared with his father. He called his sizable poem a Song, and at one time inserted himself in the heavenly Chorus with his contribution. That is why I suggested at the beginning you read him aloud as much as you can.

Do not expect him to spend much time counting syllables. He had practiced the art of poetry since his gifted childhood. His early work shows him adept in a variety of verse forms. His Latin verse gave him a sense of symmetry, and his knowledge of the language added depth of meaning to his own English usage. Latin formality appears in Adam and Eve's manner of addressing each other as Lord and Lady of the Land with only one condition to observe. It seemed easy at the time to resist the forbidden fruit when they had such abundance in its place. Notice how the tone changes as their familiarity grows. How simple the "celestial Colloquy sublime" becomes as God teases Adam about wanting a mate.

Latin constructions such as "human face divine" and Hell burning "frore" [frozen] challenge the reader to experience opposites as one. My favorite oxymoron is "palpable obscure" for its dimensions of response.

Milton's knowledge of ancient Semitic languages, particularly biblical Hebrew, provides the poem with its many constructions in biblical style—parallel structure, repetition, rhythms, and balanced opposites of light and dark, night and day, heaven and earth, wet and dry, all addressing the duality of the universe, all finally absorbed into the Judaic God of Glory.

As an idealist, Milton was drawn to contemporary Neoplatonism. The archangel Raphael represents the appeal character values "by gradual scale sublim'd" had for him. To say more on this subject is beyond the scope of this book. As a religious poet, Milton chose to climb the patriarch Jacob's ladder, each step "mysteriously meant" to the summit, with Holy Spirit's help pursuing the "best and noblest things."

To explore the sources of thought and imagination is an act of the intellect, Milton wrote elsewhere. To believe in God is an action of the heart. After long "self debatements," in the vibrant air of thought, he arrived at an inner holiness which spoke privately for the soul. Didactically, the key word is "obedience." To obey is to love. To love is to obey. "The love I have in mind is love of God," Milton explains, "and not only the love which arises from the instinct and awareness of the love which he has for us." Invisible presence. We converse. We cannot live without him. Spiritual substance, not material reality. In his time he will reveal himself fully. Meanwhile, he is dependable wisdom in whom we are wise.

Who can explain the *creative process*? Where did those wonderful metaphors come from? The brilliantly rendered tropes within a trope? (See the first anthology piece, "With Thee Conversing.") How did the internal rhyme appear at just the right time? Milton is so dazzling in invention, one forgets some hard-working facts, some hard-won knowledge from experience may be part of the technique of poetry as well as the metaphysical imagination. In addition, the didactic matter cannot be overlooked as a bonding element of theme and structure. Above all, answerable to his style is the way in which he sounds what he sees and feels, as if his words were set to music on every page. A style uniquely his. He would call it Holy Spirit. I call it a perfect ear for sound, a rich source of language in mind and memory for meaning. Behind the words, other words, intimations, echoes.

The Creation of the World
Giusto de' Menabuoi
1370-1378
Baptistry, Padua, Italy

CREATING THE WORLD

Who has not been spellbound by Genesis I? Who has not in some way been affected by its austere style, its sheer persuasion, its authority, its poetry, the very look of the letters on the page? "In the beginning God created heaven and earth." What is more convincing though unprovable? More reverential? More simple though far from simple? Milton speculated with philosophers, mathematicians, rabbis, Church Fathers, Scripture itself. The more he searched himself and others for answers, the more dithyrambic he became. God's manifesting himself in time and space is no mere amplification of Genesis but the phenomenal effect of his "overshadowing spirit and might" on the poet, a master of imagination, insight, inspiration, invention, and technical ability of the highest order.

"Creation is the act by which God the Father produced everything that exists by his word and spirit," Milton tells us elsewhere. In striking contrast to religious poets who attempted full dramatization of the Week, Milton's remains the most ardent account of the "enormous bliss" of creativity in action, from the sublime to genial humor in the smallest observed homely detail. God's "great Idea" lives abundantly, jubilantly. Yesterday. Tomorrow. Today.

"Let there be light." So God spoke. So his compass materialized his words. Lesser lights followed—sun, moon, stars and mist before the rains to keep the garden at its freshest—felicities of Paradise, fruit and flower. Earth as early as the third day was a "seat where Gods might dwell or wander with delight." Heaven and earth were equipped with necessary natural elements. Milton expands Genesis, elaborates, delights, enriches through dynamic painterly imagery and volatility of process that move from source into substance, by day from grand style to sheer homely detail of the smallest creature described.

Stately trees rise as in a dance. Fish "sporting with quick glance / Show to the Sun thir wav'd coats dropt with Gold." How breathtaking the multiplying of animal births, immediately active, energetic assertions of life each after its own kind, each with its due proportion of divine breath. They "also know,/ And reason not contemptibly." "The emmet (ant) in small room large heart enclos'd." So the soul came into the world.

> Was ever passive voice used so pictorially?
>> Air, Water, Earth
> By fowl, fish, Beast, was flown, was swum, was walkt
> Frequent.

I think of Tintoretto's *Creation of the Animals*. It is a wonderful study in movement. Milton's art ranges from dynamic splendor to just plain, enjoyable whimsy. He uses all his poetic means—painting, music, architecture; his intellectual and his whole sensual apparatus to surprise and delight.

Uriel, the great angel of light, asks, "Of such mystery who can tell?" Milton tells, out of the power of his faith and gratitude to God.

The Creation of Man
Michelangelo Buonarroti
1508-1512
Sistine Chapel, Vatican Palace
Vatican City, Italy

THE CREATION OF ADAM

There yet remained to be created that creature "with Sanctity of Reason . . . upright with Front serene . . . self-knowing . . . and from thence / Magnanimous to correspond with Heav'n" (VII. 508-11). It's a tall order, and what is important is "self-knowing"—an inwardness that encapsulates the mystery of origin and "the matter-of-fact of a life lived toward the mark of meaningful values in the context of God's whole purpose for it, a life full of joy, energy, spirit, and the fun of getting into the stream of being, breaking through trials and griefs to the happiness that makes men "thrice happy" to know.

Adam, recounting what he remembered of his birth to Raphael (VIII), found himself on his back among flowers, his first sight the sky. He contemplated it briefly, then: sprang to his feet: He asked the Sun and the Earth it "enlight'n'd"; asked all in their place, and the living, moving, flying "who I was, or where, or from what cause":

> Tell if ye saw, how came I thus, how here?
> Not of myself; by some great Maker then,
> In goodness and in power preeminent;
> Tell me how I may know him, how adore,
> From whom I have that thus I move and live,
> And feel that I am happier than I know.
>
> (VIII. 277-282)

Milton had the early Judaic awe toward Adam, for on him God "set on man his equal love" (VIII. 282). Doubtless Milton draws on his own experience of the "Vision bright" to advance his instinctive sense of a higher power in his consciousness.

Is awareness of God a response to an ancient, inexplicable need or the instigation of it? Is that need something residual in the imagination we, paradoxically, make up? Until God himself proves himself beyond our guesses and inventions, we cannot know why the surge upward is there, the instinctive pull to mountain summits, hills, symbolic heights of God's moral and metaphysical excellence create in us such inner happiness.

Exhausted with his unanswered questions, Adam once more falls asleep. A disturbance of air, a sense as of flying—"smooth sliding without step": Adam is carried from the great garden of his origin to his smaller but no less beautiful new home and authority. "A shape Divine," "an inward apparition," a voice. Recognizing Deity, with awe and joy, he fell to the ground in the old style, prone. And then that packed, passionate, thrilling line:

> Submiss: he rear'd me, and Whom thou sought'st I am.
>
> (VIII. 316)

Stories of Genesis
Relief by Lorenzo Maitani
1320
Cathedral, Orvieto, Italy

MANLIKE, BUT DIFFERENT SEX

Creation of Eve

Calmed down from the heady heights of the "celestial Colloquy sublime," (VIII. 455), Adam, with enormous respect and daring, asks God for a wife suitably one of his kind. God, genial now, and teasing, endearing, responds he has had one in mind all along.

Soon Adam is asleep, but under a heavenly sort of anesthesia, is able to see everything going on. Blood streamed from the incision to his side, but as with the angels in heaven, "with flesh fill'd up and healed."

> Under his forming hands a Creature grew
> Manlike, but different sex, so lovely fair,
> That what seem'd fair in all the World, seem'd now
> Mean, or in her summa up, in her contain'd
> And in her looks, which from that time infus'd
> Sweetness into my heart, unfelt before,
> And into all things from her Air inspir'd
> The spirit of love and amorous delight.
>
> (VIII. 470-77)

Eve, under the guidance of an Unseen Presence taking her to Adam, falls in love with her image in water they pass. Her first impression of Adam is not favorable: "Less winning soft, less amiably mild," and she tries to break free. But Adam is too quick for her:

> Part of my Soul I seek thee, and thee claim
> My other half; . . .

39

Eve responds:

> . . . with that thy gentle hand
> Seiz'd mine, I yielded, and from that time see
> How beauty is excell'd by manly grace
> And wisdom, which alone is truly fair.
>
> (VII. 477-491)

From his wedding day on, she is his inseparable "solace dear," his adored "other half," "his dearer half," "his consort," his "one flesh" by marriage rite freely and happily given, his delightful companion with whom to talk things over at the end of a perfect day. The difference between the sexes gives life its dynamic and drama, and literature its endless interest: our flesh by folly lost, by merciful judgment retrieved.

To Satan, newly arrived in Paradise, they were a handsome pair,

> For contemplation hee and valor form'd,
> For softness shee and sweet attractive Grace,
> Hee for God only, she for God in him.
>
> (IV. 297-299)

The Archangel Raphael
Neopolitan sculptor
16th century
Los Angeles County Museum of Art
Los Angeles, California, USA

ON THE HEIGHTS WITH RAPHAEL

Adam saw him first. A seraph straight from the throne of God. Two wings covered his face, two his feet, and two were just closing in from the flight. He spread "enormous bliss" as he moved. The angel guard was in a flurry over his high rank. His colors dazzled as if it were morning again. Eve looked up, but did not come at Adam's call. She went on with lunch, adding for a third. Juiced grapes from the vine, scooped meat from nuts and berries, made bowls of gourds (cupped hands for clean water). Flowers for a centerpiece. Hospitality was her happiness.

It was their first official visit from a heavenly messenger. Adam greeted him with simple dignity, she with a gracious-lady smile.

Up a rise, by a song brook, they sat "recline." Adam, solicitous for his guest and seeking knowledge as well, asked if a heavenly creature accustomed to airy foods could accommodate coarser earth greens. Eve listened with interest. Something new to talk about when she and Adam reviewed events of the day. Besides, transformation from the never-ending produce of the garden was her special area of interest as preparer of meals.

As she moved about with second helpings, she was aware of the way the two looked at her, Adam adoringly, Raphael uncertainly. She had expected more warmth from the angel in response to her smile, for to please gave her pleasure.

From the garden, as she worked, she heard the two talking. Raphael had a fund of entertaining stories, all promising the good life, "If thou be found obedient." Adam bristled at any thought he could break his pledge to God. To obey is to love. To love is to obey. The message was clearly meant for Adam and Eve. The enemy had been sighted in Paradise, and all the earth must be on guard.

Sometimes she wondered why God and the great angels, with all their power of word and act, couldn't wipe him out in a breath.

She dozed off, then alerted to the sound of her name. Heard herself praised as a gift of God—the "wisest, virtuousest, discreetest, best." Not even Adam's endearing qualifications—"Those thousand decencies that daily flow / From all her words and actions, mixt with Love . . . which declare unfeign'd / Union of Mind . . . one Soul"—spared Adam the reprimand of uxoriousness and carnality. Then, as if to make up for his harshness, on taking leave, the angel generously suggested that Adam attempt to reach an exalted status like his own. That is, if he is obedient.

Climb Jacob's ladder (every step mysteriously meant) to the sublime, shared with Raphael's scale "till body up to spirit work." Expand with Milton's imagination and inspiration as he makes his way through to knowledge and from there on to the heart. Harmony is the key word in his spiritual goal of man, nature, cosmos one with God, time and eternity one in the fullness of faith.

Raphael's way of achieving "Union of Pure with Pure" is a Christianized Platonism. Eve did not know what heights she was destined for, but without Adam to clear her divided mind, to beckon her to bed sweetly at night, to seek her hand whatever she was doing by day, without Adam—no happiness. Likewise, should God approve Adam for those heights, without Eve—no happiness, unless God give her to him again.

To the archangel Raphael, who had come to put Adam on alert against Satan, Eve was "the weaker" (not Milton's word, but the apostle Peter's, in his first letter 3:7), and Raphael warns Adam not to exaggerate his wife's merits.

However, my portrait of Eve is best expressed in the exquisite simplicity of God's loving kindness he chose when presenting her to Adam:

> What next I bring shall please thee, be assured,
> Thy likeness, thy fit help, thy other self
> Thy wish exactly to thy heart's desire.
>
> (VIII. 449-451)

Did God overlook some truths of feminine psychology? Or did He think too highly of Adam?

SATAN: HERO OR HELLER?

When Milton, in the tradition of the classical epics, began his poem in the midst of things, the war in heaven was over. But not for Satan. Day after day,—night after night he and his rebel angels fell—time enough to plan his revenge on God, who had never given him any occasion for bitterness. He lies in hellfire burning cold. Soon Pandemonium rises for Parliamentary discourse and from his gaudy throne he manages to get himself elected for the dangerous mission to the new heaven on earth. So the book opens with a fall from grace like that of the human pair later, but without their opportunity for redemption.

He begins his long, perilous venture, upborne out of the "dark, unbottom'd, infinite abyss."

> Dropping, rebounding,
> O'er bog or steep, through strait, rough, dense, or rare,
> With head, hands, wings, or feet pursues his way.
> And swims or sinks, or wades, or creeps, or flies.

His mind a chaos like the chaos he clears, he pours out his thoughts in an extended soliloquy to the elements, arguing incoherently, justifying his ambition to replace God with at best a hollow and temporary victory. Thrashing about in petulance and hurt feelings, he makes his decision. "Evil, be thou my good." Angel of light illuminated no longer.

Milton's portrait of Satan is so convincing in the early books, that some readers downplay Milton's irony for heroic resistance to a tyrant who himself brought evil into the world out of the dark hole in his pocket and permitted until Satan exposed his self-aggrandizement in the war. Perversely, they see him as protagonist of the poem. They admire him for his courage against seemingly insurmountable odds. But hero he is not. In the Invocation to Book IX Milton tells us the true hero is a man of virtue who is ever in building his character toward perfection, living life as God would have us do, in love and gratitude for the music and order of the laws, accepting happiness as the sum of sorrows and celebration, the daily fare received with patience and fortitude.

Roughed up and bluffing his way, full of hate, envy and malice, Satan reaches earth. Approaching Eden like a sightseer, he sees the wide passage where "Over the Promised Land to God so dear," angels are to take messages to man. He stands on the lower rung of the ladder where the patriarch Jacob dreamed he saw angels ascending and descending. "Each stair was mysteriously meant." I live by that line. He is struck with wonder at "the sudden view of this world all at once."

Oh for the maturity early enough to see the pattern of our lives clearly and in the wisdom and vision of the holy build for the Paradise lost the Paradise within! Then on into the breathtaking garden itself (Milton never stints praising Nature for doing her part), the peaceable animals, the innocent lovers in their bower; "Wonderful indeed are all his works."

Crouching in the Tree of Life, he contemplates doing "what else though damned I should abhor." At Eve's ear he implants his sordid dream until tracked by angel sentries, alerted to his Identity. Noble or nefarious? How did they know him as impostor? That distorted face had no serenity of spirit in it.

The Expulsion from the Garden of Eden
Emilian school
17th century
Pinaoteca, Civiche Raccolte d'Arte Antica
del Castello Storzesco
Milan, Italy

THE FALL AND AFTER

1.

Eve had a dream. Tree of death, but the fruit was alive on her mouth, and good. No guilt where no intention, Adam consoled her. But a wife does not tell her husband everything on her mind. He was concerned. In his arms she thought of another's. What if she only walked up to the tree, looked, and walked away? A little absence reluctantly permitted. Back by noon.

Tears. Torment. Everybody knows the story. It reads like a novel, unfolds like the eternal drama of a man and woman locked in loathing as intense as their love still was. "Out of my sight, thou Serpent!" His dearer half! Exhausted from their ordeal, they agreed to return to the place where God had judged them and ask forgiveness. I have always had a special fondness for those intrepid little travelers, their prayers, that braved contrary winds to arrive straight in heaven and unerringly make their way to God's throne. And God, who had withdrawn the death sentence, was once more merciful.

2.

Nothing is ever lost but that is found again where left, deep in a recess of mind. So it was with an epic poem Milton had tried years before to make sing and could not. Now the time had come when he set off buoyantly on a major poem—"something unattempted yet in Prose or Rhyme." Edward Phillips, his nephew and pupil, gives the date as about two years before the Restoration of the young prince to his crown in 1660. No conditions were attached. The Puritans had a passion for probity, and morals at court were deplorable. Humbly Milton asks for help from Holy Spirit and is soon blessed with Celestial Light to take the place of his blind eyes. He was writing as well as ever with the help of Holy Spirit. But personal anxieties as to his health and political uneasiness about his sentence as friend and defender of the men who brought about the execution of Charles I was distracting. However his sentence was light—a brief imprisonment, a fine, freedom to call them Heroes.

He must now turn his notes to tragic. Adam and Eve must leave Paradise already breaking up, the climate changing, the gentle animals becoming hostile. The first great angel God sent, Raphael, instructed Adam on the bright spiritual heights of a life scaled to perfection. "Be strong, live happy, and love, but first of all / Him whom to love is to obey" (VIII, 633-634). God's choice for the second, Michael, is serious, sympathetic, down-to-earth. "Dismiss them not disconsolate," God in his concern advises.

In dreamlike images of the ancient past, the archangel depicts the ruthless drive of men for wealth, power and slaves. In addition, he narrates pertinent events from Jewish history, pausing at the divine laws of Moses, which, despite their great contribution to personal morality and stable government the world over, could only locate evil, not prevent it. God is patient. He will not forget his faithful. "To create / Is greater than created to destroy" (VII. 605. He promises an eternity of "all things new/ Both Heaven and Earth wherein the just shall dwell." (XI. 900-901).

Meanwhile, the composite portrait of humanity is disheartening for corruption, disease, lowered values. The archangel makes no attempt to soften the grim truth. "So shall the World go on," he admits, "to good malignant, to bad men benign" to which Adam, after some confusion, responds in a creed for all churches, free of dogmatic differences and discontents, in as simple and beautiful an English as Milton ever wrote, and as devout.

3.

The flaming red signal appears in the sky. Adam and Eve, with humble dignity, thank their divine instructor and, joining hands as at the beginning, God-clothed against the cold, depart in words as plain and unforgettable as they are.

Hardly a visible boundary between the shambles they had made of Paradise and the world before them, wild, unknown, yet offering all possible. Genesis tells us Eve was home to generations of children. Adam lived his long years a silent man and, I believe, a holy one.

For both, God was, will be, and always is our Creator who helps us bear the bitterness of life for the wonder of the sweet; who raises us from low to high and higher realms of spirit as we can to give us a good and happy life till we live with him again in gratitude and grace.

Judgment Day (detail)
Pietro Cavallini
c. 1293
Santa Cecilia in Trastevere
Rome, Italy

ANGELS, COME CLOSE

Angels have been on man's mind since mind first became conscious of itself and the mystery of being human. My study of other cultures and religious systems has led to respect for basic similarities and a humble, deeper engagement with my own.

True angels are spirit, the presence of God in the world, the idea of the celestial in us. We can never explain what they are or why certain of us believe beyond reason. But we can be richer human beings in understanding them reverentially.

The greatest source of Judeo-Christian angels is the Bible and non-canonical writings associated with it. I grew up on legends that improve in understanding with time. The God of our fathers, and of us, was one of three men-angels who came to eat at Abraham's table. He imaged himself as a burning bush and a pillar of fire. He wrestled with Jacob all night, and for Jacob's courage, promised him a new name and a great destiny. A ladder leaning against a house creates for me a dreaming Jacob, seeing angels ascending and descending, linking earth and heaven. The incident never loses its beauty for me as a metaphor of union with God. To go from the sublime to the ridiculous—though it is not so ridiculous as it appears—even Balaam's ass knew an angel when he stopped for one crossing his lowly path. Milton said of the animals he created, "They reason not contemptibly."

In the book of his name, Daniel writes of his extraordinary experience. "While I was speaking in prayer, the man Gabriel [an archangel whose name means 'Thought of God'] who I had seen in the vision at the beginning, being caused to fly swiftly, touched-me."

Michael, another archangel, is shared by several traditions. On earth he is a prince and warrior; in heaven, holder of the keys and weigher of souls. How can angels be in two worlds at the same time? Ask the quantum physicist how particles can pass into each other right through barriers between them.

Angel means "messenger," from the 'Greek "angelos." The Hebrew word is *mal'akh*, which also means "messenger," but originally meant "the shadow side of God." I like that, and I like St. Augustine's "indwelling." I'm humbled by the thought I'm entertaining an angel within. Fallen angels take us into ethics and the problem of evil. My angels have their being in a spiritual dimension, who relate us to a higher level of existence. Angels are spirit, and we are partly spirit. So we connect, and from there on, angel to angel in the depths of our soul, we touch each other, good to good, one to one.

Angels are not Grecian goddesses in flowing robes. They are not cute little charmers that started with Raphael's *putti* and continue as Cupids and cherubs, belly button and genitals showing in layers of fat. (How the mighty cherubim around God's throne have been "belittled!"). They are not idealized likenesses of human beings. They have their own character as ideas. They are not New Age softies who will deliver whatever you want. Angels are not, as dour Karl Barth calls them, "curiosities of our invention." They are not optical illusions caused by the mind's fatigue. No representation of them can come close to the real thing because no one knows what the real thing is.

Wings vary in numbers depending on what prophet has the vision. The patriarch Enoch acquired thirty-six when he was translated highest in the angel hierarchy. Raphael appeared to Adam and Eve in the feathered glory of six. Rilke writes that the least flapping of wings would beat you to death. Wings are emblems of God's power and stir the imagination.

Angels have so long been known in the world's cultures, it is hard to deny them a certain kind of truth. There is a wonderfulness that those of us who believe in them share without being able to explain except on grounds of special attunement to sacred legends and an imagination for things that are past understanding. That is not to say one closes one's mind to problems associated with non-material beings. Of course outcroppings of wings of whatever number are anatomically impossible; unaided body flights of bodiless creatures are fantasy; heavenly rescues are wishful thinking. Angels are metaphors—and sublime ones—for deep truths that legends come closer to conveying than logic. They lie deep in our subconscious. A sound and reverent intuition allows us through them to transcend earthly limitations for unearthly gains of spirit. In the end, a mystery.

The great period of religious art was for us the late Middle Ages through the Renaissance to seventeenth-century Rembrandt. Let the holiness that surrounds celestial beings speak to you from the pages of very fine collections. The modern period is not favorable to angels. Artists view them as sad, sick, wounded. Klee's angels emerge from a wrecked Paradise, uncomfortable in the world, mere whimsies. On the other hand, Marc Chagall's people and animals celebrate their joy in life where no laws of gravity apply.

Gustav Davidson's *A Dictionary of Angels* is fascinating to browse. In my early edition I learned that there are 301,677,722. According to Jewish tradition, angels are new every morning and continue to be formed with every breath God takes. "Millions of spiritual creatures walk the Earth / Unseen, both when we wake, and when we sleep." Milton invented a few, himself.

I believe angels have no visible substance but have their being deep within us and answer to a need for the good and noble in life. They stimulate our imagination, persuade us of spiritual forces in the world. In our unknowing, we give thanks for what we know.

FAITHFUL CHAMPION, GLORIOUS WITNESS

Whatever learned projects remained in draft, the three poems that had lain so long in his mind were finished. *Paradise Regained* and *Samson Agonistes* followed publication of' *Paradise Lost.* Very little of Milton's correspondence has survived. Much reduced in income since the Restoration, he lived his last years in the simplest of his lifetime lodgings—a house that had one room to a floor. Ever vital himself, despite physical ailments, he enjoyed the support of his young, companionable wife, Elizabeth Minshull, who helped him finish his various writing projects for publication and capably managed his house and health, joked with him, and, above all, was kind.

Visitors left him with good conversation or exchanges of choice poets. Others came to Bread Street, his birthplace destroyed by the Great Fire, or to Artillery Row to catch sight of the renowned scholar and—more recently—the epic poet. Revisions had been asked for a new edition if *Paradise Lost,* externals chiefly, and they were made. He ate simply and retired early. He woke in dark to be in light.

Senility never approached his vigorous opinions and constantly renewed powers. He lived between remembrance and anticipation. Hobbes raised his hackles, but he respected Hobbes's right to his maimed reality. He was scornfully amused at the kind of flashy heroism Dryden asked to exploit his *Paradise Lost* for. Spenser was closer to Waller sitting before him.

He went from one life to another so imperceptibly, so quietly apart, the exact time is his secret, not known and never will be. To read the last poems is to have an understanding of what time it was, what sort of light he was in when taken.

Death was interwoven with the living of his life—his mother in 1637, Charles Diodati the following year, relatives, good friends, wives, his infant son. And his beloved father. Death in *Paradise Lost* first appears as a shadowy fear—as a product of Satan, a future without hope. But in the religious context of love, death becomes "the gate of life," as it was for Adam in his long life. And for Samson in his sublimation. And for Milton as he ended what the anonymous biographer calls "so Christian a life." Chiefly I think of him in those last days and hours so serene no one thought to mark them.

How far from those in the room. How far from war and plague, death carts rumbling in the street on their way to the plague-pit, death bells, division. How near the early years when he was learning Hebrew, enchanted by the mysterious dignity of the letters themselves, awesome in their firmness yet giving off an aura of divinity compounded by their grouping into words.

Who was in the room? Was his friend Dr. Paget with him? His attentive wife? His devoted brother Christopher? Was it the 8th? 9th? 10th? In early November, sometime within a month of his sixty-sixth birthday, he died "with so little pain" (the anonymous biographer tells us) "that the time of his expiring was not perceived by those in the room." Masson gives the date as November 8, late at night; A.N. Wilson as November 9. No one knows. He died as if he were translated like his favorite Elijah, quietly without a date, perhaps on the verge of new lines to dictate, not for us to hear unless, believers, we hear his light, tuneful voice in the heavenly chorus. "His harmonical and ingenious soul did lodge in a beautiful and well-proportioned body." For all the things Aubrey set down to check, he makes that statement without further inquiry.

He was received in the name of the church by the curate and was buried November 12, 1674, at St. Giles Cripplegate, his parish church. And I think he would have had no objection to the Church of England service for the occasion, for its words are one of the "elegances of life" he never lost his taste for in his battle with the "blind mouths" that only mouthed them.

How far the mourners in procession. "All his learned and great friends in London, nor without a friendly concourse of the Vulgar"—the word is not used pejoratively—"accompanied his body to the church." Possibly some sightseers, too, were present, for they had begun to come to Bread Street, where his birth house had been destroyed in the Great Fire—"the hoorible, malicious, bloody flame, not like the fine flame of an ordinary fire," Pepys wrote. How right they should pay their respects to the faithful champion and glorious witness of God.

How suitable the words of 11 Chron. 31:21: "And in every work that he began in the service of the house of God, and in the law, and in the commandments, to seek his God, he did it with all his heart." How right that burial was with his father. Some time later, parts of the poet's body were dug up and sold for relics. But by then, Holy Spirit had returned him to "Empyreal Air" for good.

SOMETHING UNATTEMPTED

Milton's announced aesthetic purpose is to "pursue/Things unattempted yet in Prose or Rhyme." The Invocations to Book 1, III, VII and questionably IX, are musing on his deepest religious experience. Prayerfully contemplative rather than purely petitionary or penitential, they are holy conversations on the projected and advancing poem. Spaced like piers supporting the poem, they reach to the one God in the swirling lyric dance that makes them seem in movement while standing firm, out of inner stillness.

Invocation I, which I have placed in the anthology section, is notable for its virtuosity.

> What in me is dark
> Illumine, what is low raise and support
> That to the highth of this great Argument
> I may assert Eternal Providence,
> And justify the ways of God to man.
>
> (I. 22-26)

The tone is humble yet tenacious. One is reminded of Jacob wrestling with God at Peniel. "I will not let thee go, except thou bless me" (Gen. 32.36).

Visit and *Revisit* echo throughout Invocation III with the immediacy and venturesome of flight. Ascent plays against descent, light against dark, union against separation. Milton sees light metaphorically as a "sovran vital lamp." Whether that light existed from Eternity as God or was created like other secondarily like other created things made no difference. "Eternal Coeternal beam" or "pure Ethereal stream," it flows from the giver to receiver and makes them one. The approach to Holy Spirit is delicate and reverent, gauged to precise but intense feelings.

The greater part of this Invocation concerns his blindness, and it contains some of the most beautiful lines in the poem. "Smit with the love of sacred Song," he frequents old familiar places, but misses their fullness to physical sight: gardens, "the human face divine," and "wisdom at one entrance" blocked out. But his gain is greater for the internal vision it gives him, and he asks for its illumination to continue.

> So much the rather thou Celestial light
> Shine inward, and the mind through all her powers
> Irradiate, there plant eyes, all mist from thence
> Purge and disperse, that I may see and tell
> Of things invisible to mortal sight.
>
> (III. 51-55)

I am reminded of a line by Anthony Hecht: "A light so pure and just." If, to some, Milton's dwelling on his loss of sight seems self-indulgent, I find him straightforward and earnest. He is awesomely aware of the power of an all-illuminating and holy Spirit and his indebtedness to it in the petitioning of his heart. I am thinking of a line in Saint Augustine: "You raised me up so that I could see that there was something to see and that I still lacked the ability to see it."

Invocation VII brings him to the halfway point of his song. This Holy Spirit answers his prayer.

> Up led by thee
> Into the Heav'n of Heav'ns I have presumed,
> An Earthly Guest and drawn Empyreal Air,
> Thy temp'ring.
>
> (VII. 12-15)

But the tone turns elegiac as, back on Earth, he is distraught by the "barbarous dissonance" of the Restoration court, so much in contrast to the Puritan ideal of conduct.

Some do not consider the introduction to Book IX a fourth Invocation, but it is often treated so in discussion. This illuminating Spirit still visits him nightly, but will it bring him the style needed for the darkening of the text? Obstacles affecting personal sensibility must be overcome: the times, the winter cold, his advancing age. No doubt there are more he does not enumerate, such as the frustrations of blindness, the pain of gout, the snarls in the reduction of word to idea, nerves acting up, the usual fears of an author faced with a turn his subject matter is to take in a new direction. He is particularly worried that his readers may not understand his meaning of Heroic Martyrdom, which he defines as "the better fortitude / Of Patience and Heroic Martyrdom." He makes it clear that he does not mean a brutal Achilles or a gaudy knight in meaningless tournament. From the time conjectured for this work, I would say he meant men like the regicides who gave their lives for what was right and good. He, himself, as a friend fared better in court. "What harm can an old man do?" scoffed Charles II.

"Disobedience" of Invocation I locks into "disobedience" of early Book IX. His Muse, that abiding Spirit of light, gives him his "answerable style." His anxieties vanish. He makes the turn. He continues on the graver course. He puts it in its divine context with concrete vividness, personal intensity, integrity of commitment, and the holy art of the Bible itself.

**Portrait of John Milton engraved by Robert White
for the fourth edition of** *Paradise Lost*
Printed by Miles Flesher for Jacob Tonson, London, 1688
Courtesy of Rauner Library, Dartmouth College

IV

MILTON ON MY MIND: A TRIBUTE

MILTON ON MY MIND

> To create/ Is greater than created to destroy.
> —Milton, *Paradise Lost*

Milton! You should be living at this hour:
Our poetry goes nowhere going new.
Not trends but inner Paradise your power.
What we have lost in obsolescing you!

You made an old verse line speak rare and strong.
Winged in flight for another end of flight
You gave your heart and tempered ear to song.
Blind, you kept the holy in plain sight.

You knew first hand heckled Samson's pain.
The stones you walked were Adam's sacred-places.
You showed that happiness had to contain
Earth's bitter-sweet and heaven's sunlit traces.

You readied night thoughts for a later hand
In joy of words for all created things.
You sounded Gloria in anthems grand
Or soft, your shelter warm celestial wings.

Winter brought best verse, heart whole, hands numb.
You smelled the stench of court and man and Thames,
But you resisted, venturesome,
Your blind eyes leading into light like gems.

You matched your words to music voiced at dawn,
Sitting like crystal in the sun, shone on.
To live well is to say of the Sublime
No one lives unloved in time to come, or time.

THOUGHTS ON GUSTAV DAVIDSON'S
A DICTIONARY OF ANGELS

1.

Though the
mind has no place
in Grey's *Anatomy*
Is that any reason not to
use it?

If life's
a dream and we
its captive audience,
shouldn't we try to stay awake
longer?

Why should
matter-of-faith
be plagued with doubt? Even
science makes uncertainty its
last word.

With so
much evidence
before us, can there not
be some factual substance to
belief?

2.

Aspects
of God become
angels of his presence.
Call any by their name and you
call him.

3.

Out of
dense spruce branches
flash of blue in flight. Don't
mistake a bird on wing for an
angel.

Angels
metabolize
weightless for long distance.
Watch close for what is bright enough
to mean.

4.

Where were
they when I fell
last week? The week before?
The voice is firm but kind: "Take care.
Read or

walk—not
both," she warns with
clear authority. Still
I'm a breeze common sense can't slow
or save.

A FEW WORDS

With God
every breath is
an angel: with angels.
their every word is *hineni*—
"Send me."

Father,
may I serve you
all my life, flying a
little lower than angels,
a blue bird.

PERSUADED

Whether
angels come rarely
or are always here,

Whether
they are assigned errands
or simply volunteer,

Whether
some are so high in rank
they never appear,
but stand about the throne,
glory their career,

Whether
they reflect true light
in their own form clear,
or manifest as pure forces
of crystal atmosphere,

Whether
holiday bound earthward
or resident all year,

I believe I believe
in what's beyond, and near.

Ida Fasel

GENESIS

What heights,
what story plots,
what unforgettable
characters, what epic grandeur
simple

statements
make, what lyric
sound their holy music
on pulses in poem after
poem!

Later,
Daniel could name
the angel in his room,
but nameless come with messages
as well

people
who look like us
but recognizably
loftier, and who knows which one
is God?

BE STILL

. . . and know that I am.
—Psalm 46:10

Tented
in Mamre shade,
Abraham saw three forms
approaching in a golden haze.
At once

he fell
to his knees. How
did he know which of the
three was God? How did he know he
was right?

TRUE FREEDOM IS SIGNIFICANT BONDAGE

Those depth rabbis poring over the Talmud
trapped in what they know
   they do not know
lingering over poems embedded in poems
will put up with all the nitty gritty
   of just and realistic principles
and round up all the possibilities
to make sure they don't miss
   whatever might be on the sacred mind
showing through at the glorious edge
   of human limits.
A life to cling to for dear life.
A sea that holds you up if you let it
   be your spine.
A planet losing its blue to bluer
   the farther you leave it.
The word for which there is no word
   for the worth.
Hour after hour
in a gray interior
pearly from the sun's rays
held shimmering in the narrow windows
passing, swiftly passed—
they walk the fine line of the text
   finer for wear
and approach
   the hand not free to touch
   the sight forbidden to have.
More than meets the eye, their bearings.

PATTERNS

Our love of patterns proves we were created.
Designs complex or simple tell us so.
We are by Genesis illuminated,

By geometry and compass antedated.
Not for us the random embryo.
Our love of patterns proves we were created,

From curves and angles never separated
Colors give austerity a glow.
We are by Genesis illuminated,

Our origin with reverence narrated.
To poetry of ancient ink we owe
Our love of patterns, proof we were created

And with a serious purpose elevated
Into a vaster design than we can know.
We are by Genesis illuminated,

Its matchless words draw us from the debated:
The Big Bang guess is not our way to go.
Our love of patterns proves we were created.
We are by Genesis illuminated.

Ida Fasel

THANKFUL

At the first breakthrough of life,
thank ground for winter care.
Thank stem and leaf for risking
life and finding it good.
Thank hyacinths standing tall.
Thank anemones delicately braving
the wind. Thank crocus
unintimidated by snow.

Thank the lady who said Yes
to a clipping of Old Blush.
Thank my patient husband
who waited out the stop-and-start
of weary search. He too loves
a garden steadied by
the oldest flower in it.

Is that a honeybee
reconnoitering so early?
Thank whatever you think it is.
Thank the hummer hovering
at red tulip's door. Is he saying
Stopping by but can't stay?
but stays anyway on wings that keep him
aloft while he visits, complete
with refreshments, and his restless
energy holds him in what looks
like pure rest before he darts off,
bearing away on his wings
the future life of a flower.

Thank spring for day's
happy returns. Thank the lark.
taking to heaven our gratitude, his song.

GRATITUDE FOR MY HUSBAND'S HAND

Thy gentle hand/ Seiz'd mine.
Paradise Lost, IV. 489-490

Gently
your hand seized mine
holding hard against the
uneven path. From that day on,
I learned

how quick
to care a firm
hand is, how slight the pain
of harm's way shared, so glad by you
to stand.

Ida Fasel

THE WINDOW AS MEDITATION

Frost on
the window pane—
little by less whittled
away—the morning sun at its
busy

routine—
spring approaching:
As if they had never
been—all these beautiful strange beasts
wiped clean!

THE BRIGHT SIDE

I believe in what is absurd—Tertullian

Those days
were like getting
a letter from the world
signed in his own hand "Will Shakespeare."
Like a

wind that
picks you up and
dances you out of sight.
Like being a tree, ancient of
days, young

of crown,
busy with breath
works for all who need to
breathe. As the present turns past, will
you trust

my skewed
truth, silent on
the way things were and
are, still believing I have the
last word,

bounding
buoyant waters,
glistening fine powdered,
raising a friendly storm of snow
on the slopes?

THE EPHEMERAL LASTS AGAINST ALL PREDICTION

1.

Living to the end of the century
Is like living in all of it
and all the centuries that have spun earth
to its place among the stars.
The awful parts and the good coalesce
into something like a bind.
Shakespeare's Pardon's the word to all
turns to acid on the tongue.
Fellowship is more likely to be a meeting
where one side keeps talking
and the other walks out.

2.

How many stones
we skipped across this river

touching surfaces
sinking deeper than sunlight

to glow among
those that glow in the dark

rock bottom crammed
with rock

mine to yours
without rivalry

yours to mine
engagingly

from whose hand once more
a count, a wish, a song?

BELONGING

Deep in the shade and shadow of great wings
Like those of an imperial eagle, warm
As monk-enfolding wool, I take the stings
Of science, sheltered by unchanging form.
From Ptolemy to astrophysics, learning
Diminishes the earth from splendid stance
To wobbler to nonentity now burning
Out, gone all grace once seen in dance.
It may be other galaxies in space
Will last beyond our own, fit to take on
Our planet's homeless after this small place
And life support of every kind are gone.
    My trust is in a power so sublime,
     He'll bring the Week again from void to time.

CONSOLED

When I feel myself distancing
day's eye for my own dark, I go to the poet:
The world is charged with the grandeur of God.
When I try to find my way
out of the 10,000 foot deep polar ice cap
of your suffering and death,
I am encompassed
with warm breast and with ah! bright wings.
Where were they in your need?
How tirelessly Hopkins strove
with himself, with his poems, but chiefly
with that God whose mercy was his glory,
his wherefore and why, torment.

You bore my nursing with courtesy of character.
If only I had done better!
For days you no longer looked as you did.
Then you slipped away with
the last light off the black/west.

Morning springs eastward and you awake in me.

BORN TO BELIEVE

When I was a child I spake as a child . . .
but when I became a man I put away
childish things.
—1 Cor. 13:11

When Adam and Eve left Eden
they left an apple rotting in the grass,
visible bite quickly turned brown,
the tree heavy on their back.

When Adam and Eve went out of Eden
they went out from a shambles.
What was Paradise but God?
They had gone against him.

As Adam and Eve departed the familiar
a light on the ground before them
shone out steps and in those steps
they followed.

What is Paradise but the One
who never leaves off being with you?

Along the way they came to a bush
of wild ripe strawberries.
They plucked and ate in fragrant air.
Guests of God at supper,
visceral, wonderful, bitter-sweet:
children no more.

Ida Fasel

KIMBELL ART MUSEUM
FORT WORTH, TEXAS

Architect: Louis I. Kahn

I had come for Lord Leighton's young beauty,
May Sartoris, but the light met me first,
from the moment I entered, aware.
It made a way for me and with me,
warm and noble on my head.

Useless to ask what cunning management
of pressure and torsion, what problems
of load-bearing, what calculated controls
of auxiliaries and back-ups, what engineering
of windows, slots and piercings inspired
entrance of natural light fulfilling
the intentions of design, a building
livable, lovable, luminous in itself,
integral with the light within. How well

the poet-builder shaped space to spirit:
Though without presence, he wrote, it must be
considered as an offering to architecture
merely because of the wonder of its beginning.
How well the atmosphere serves those
who make this place their silent home
and those who only come to view,
outsiders sharing, the same first-day light.

WHERE THE LIGHT FALLS

(Georges de la Tour, *The Newborn Child*, Rennes)

Abruptly, out of the immense dark,
the light of a cupped candle picks out three,
holds them as they are in greater light,
in pulsations of stillness, awesome
as a Hebrew letter coming to a point,
softer, gentler, more iridescent spelled out.
They could be townspeople modeling,
or the artist's mother and his wife. The baby
could be any baby observed in newborn wonder.
More likely, Anne is directing the light to fall
from Mary to the child in her gaze and her lap.
They look as if they had been to a shrine
and wear its medal of pilgrimage in their face.

Woman, behold thy son:
head consummating the light,
eyes closed, nose a lump of unformed clay,
sleeping mouth open to what dreaming,
what saving vista in the dark surround of life?—
swaddled or shrouded, destined
to live his death forever alive,
mysterious as the sperm of spirit
that brought him into blood.

A slight smile hovers around her mouth.
Her gaze is of such benignity and grace,
the Garden might never have ceased
to be the place she was in.
How is it possible,
with only paint over paint for translucency
to create such translucency?—where the light falls,
the near sight of all that matters.

83

She gives her gaze to the child,
the artist gives his to hers
and I—I hold that gaze in my gaze.
Holy Holy Holy
Oh, I shall never be the same again,
caught in the contours of that gaze.

NUGGETS FOR A NEW CENTURY

On the mine dump of Beckett's world we still may find—
If we care enough, for it is our world, too—
Something of value the miners left behind.
His characters from birth were a hopeless crew.

If we care enough, for it is our world, too,
Day's worth is to be valued, not tossed away.
Characters from birth, a hopeless crew,
Saw themselves death-sentenced, life mere stay.

Day's worth is to be valued, not tossed away
Like fluent words askew to what is great
Though small. For those death-sentenced, life mere stay,
The dark was all, and no stone worth its weight.

No stone to cut and polish worth its weight
Left his characters a hopeless crew, blind
To some small stone whose value may prove great,
On the mine dump of Beckett's world we still may find.

>   Note: Samuel Beckett (1906-1989), Nobel Laureate,
>   whose unrelenting view of life as an existential
>   wasteland left no glimmer of the light within.

Ida Fasel

OUT OF NOTHING

Years in the millions pressed these plants to stone.
Storms took eons to calm. A single cell
Began the long division until bone
Of gilly breath lived on its own. They tell

Of molecules that formed the living power
Of unassisted generation; the bird
And tiger; grew the wheat; and shaped the plower
At history's most foreshortened point. Their word

Cannot explain the space as yet unfilled
By the emergence of clear thinking minds
Though DNA by measure of the skilled
Comes close enough to cousin our two kinds.

Flowers embedded in a stony groove
Cannot, like prayer, thorn and wing prove love.

A GLORIA FOR MILTON

Milton!
how much today
we need your pure heart, your
Just thoughts, your true ear and inner
eye, your

earthy
sublime, your calm
of ending. Blind, you were
heckled like Samson. Helped, you walked
the stones

Adam
marked where he met
God. Early to rise, you
dictated words shaped in the dark
(for day

starts, as
Genesis says,
the night before)—words like
crystal cut to be shone upon,
music

grand or
soft your glory,
celestial wings your warmth.
Milton, you should be living at
this hour!

PILGRIMAGE

I go to Shakespeare hampered all the way
By strikes from Heathrow into havoc; go
To Milton, Wordsworth, Keats pound sterling low
As my own currency. A drab wet day.
I drive my rented car in disarray,
Wrong side on winding roads out of the flow
Of tourist lines. The little left for show,
My choice, is gently yielding to decay
Or lost to steel and glass. So back to books,
Where favorites are found, alive and well.
At home I make an inner landscape mine,
Deep-hearted, hear the Highland Maid, birds, brooks;
Let truth and beauty cast their lyric spell,
With Milton follow in the *track divine*.

FRANK

From my paper world
I look over at a man named Frank
painting next door.
His slow rhythmic strokes
speak to the house as to a friend.

My Bic the right thickness and point
lies in the arch of my hand stroking time.
My green chair gives me to my work,
easy and hard, my peace and plenty,
my near-reaches—something in itself
and something to go on. It's like
talking to myself in secret and my pen
tells it the same way, pausing with me
in utter silence, softly resuming,
raising its voice to run a line through,
ardent for right meaning, right sound.

In October he will come with his
pail and Jacob's ladder to paint for me
and I, on the ladder of language,
will sometimes be taken
to the very top by angels.

Ida Fasel

AS IT WAS, AS IT IS

Wind swept to a dark, spun to a point,
sucked up, spewed, spread its waste.
Wind took our house away that night.

Looters first thing hooting past.

In the gashed open the sky
began to breathe more easily
in and out. A star. Then another.

Power down, candles began to show.
Neighbors calling to neighbors,
coming to us,
past the lilac bush intact,
jagged stone waiting for
the foundation to be firm again.

Mother stood in debris,
arms round us, voice holding close.
"My loved ones are safe."
Papa bowed his head, hands ready
for hammer and nails.

That night we too bowed earlier
than bedtime, away from our beds.

ADAM NAMING THE ANIMALS

Over the rich grains and ripe fruits,
their daily gratitude,
he intones in Hebrew letters
austere and noble—
blockbuster letters big as bells.
He rises to the high-ranging head:
Nathaniel, gift of Jehovah.
He bows to lowly loyal eyes:
Jessica, gift of Jehovah.
He kneels to the body
straining up from the ground:
Elizabeth, gift of God.
Here and here again
Immanuel and again, *Immanuel,*
God with us.

Until their children came,
children.

CREATORS

She dips
into wet clay,
getting splattered, molding,
shaping, swirling, spinning, filling
the shelf

with the
best of the lot.
I'll take the one that needs
to be thrown again, imperfect.
Like me.

CRACKING OPEN A GEODE

Behold, I will do a new thing:
now it shall spring forth.
—Isa. 43:19

First thing you must do, protect your eyes.
Splintered crystals have an edge for them.
Keep your sight for more than dust that flies:
A secret told, a lustrous favorite gem.

Or better still, let covered stone split wide
Open to the prize within. Let chisel gnaw,
Let hammer swing to amethysts each side,
Hacked and handsome even in the raw.

This rock is more than rock and must be dated
Even if no secret is revealed.
Its subtle fires can only be related
To gift of jewels as quietly concealed.

Below the cutting edge of speculation
Celebrate the bounty found in stone,
The in-depth possibles of meditation,
The music of time, the mineral in our bones.

Find inside instead the psalmist's song
An octave above the words of prayer; the glow
Of the word glow; the bush whose blue burns long,
whose light is latitant and comes on slow.

ON THE PERSISTENCE OF PARADISE

It was roundabout eighteen thousand measures,
and the name of the city from that day shall be, "The Lord is there."
—Ezek. 48:35

Tip of the bottomless past,
luminous as you look back.
Nothing like it.

Never lost:
the mind, for pleasure
    of the horizon's company perpetually
recalculates, unclenches, restores
a House of Life at the head
    of four rivers.

A myth
    obsessive, evasive
    obsolete,
word of mouth to pass along,
equal in unknowing to all the others,
all good to taste and see,
bright-lettered *P* my choice.

Nothing like it.
Paradise.
Just the sound of it
almost gets you there,
and that only in motions toward ends.
But what pure air!

City whose maker and unmaker is God.
To obey or not the overwhelming question.
Nothing like the right address.

ORIGINS

Did the universe put itself together
slowly after Big Bang sent hot chunks
flying? Or was it set in motion swiftly
once God saw first thing to be done
was to disentangle dark from light?

The story goes better, told that way.

Such possibilities!
Such a week of improbables!
Day would start in the evening.
From then on ideas multiplied,
of such fine hair they could not be
held down. Thing after thing
came into being, the sixth day
fuller in event than any day since.

On the seventh day he sat immersed
in foresight on all he had done.
The plot thickens.
Did the universe cool slowly as
its unruly free agents ranged the random
of geometer's cube and physicists' quantum?
Or did God watch the dark manifest itself
again out of bounds? And did he think

Could anyone come right up to that
buster of a no-no-tree
and see through all the foliage
between us?

On the day of rest he created grace.

Ida Fasel

ROCK HOUND

In a Chukchi legend rocks were
God's first creatures
he abandoned for a better try.

When I was small, shore rocks let me
climb them, and I talked to them
like people. They made room for me
to sit with them, shared with me
their delicacy, tangy sea-raw dulse
to eat right from where it was
planted, where I liked to be,
where the sea rushed up the rock
with a great splash and left as it
pulled back tidepools full
of tiny rocks like buttons,
and others like string, little babies
that squirmed getting the light
out of their eyes, startled awake,
alive like me.
We told each other stories.
I did most of the talking.
Time did not exist.

Here in Rocky Mountain country,
ancient seas still whisper
and rocks make wealthy rubble underfoot
or on the mountain wall itself,
where I catch the gleam of a garnet
even without cutting and polishing,
lustrous.

It tells me how earth transformed it
over long years from commonplace
to crystalline, and now the silky sheen
of its lifeblood shines through,
a little beauty of its own kind,
its own mind after all.

Ida Fasel

ANATOMY OF *PARADISE LOST*

A serious place on serious earth it is.
—Gerard Manley Hopkins

In one way it is a cathedral
going into makes a difference
for you going out—
the heart's tight fist unclenched
the ignorance of learning dispelled
the imagination stirred as if
you were given the world to name
and saw it by its meaning,
not name.

In another way it is a one-room
meeting house, walls parishioner-painted,
gleaming white, grateful annual offering.
All is open here, a happy people.

Measure for measure
the steeple divides the Sunday radiance.
Shaft of light upward,
shaft of light downward
to the outpouring of the organ
in a divine flurry, the sacred lesson
leading inward:
each in prayer as one together.

And then again it is the man,
the Puritan Poet. For the time
another is, he was.
God, Son, Satan.

all creatures of creation
from angel to ant
   in small space large heart.
and Adam who could not live
without God (building altars
wherever they talked). Adam, who
could not live without Eve.
Adam, the anthem.

In bed, running the morning's lines through
or dictating from a chair,
his bones hollowed out
to fill with eyes, voices, beings,
animals no less thought of—
   they reason not contemptibly.
Spine straight to timeless wisdom,
the constancy of love,
the wholeness of God.
Him first, him last, him midst and without end.

HEROES

When he leads his black soldiers to death,
He cannot bend his back.
—Robert Lowell

He led the charge on foot, first to be
struck in the heart: Robert Gould Shaw,
only child of fervent Boston abolitionists,
dead at 26, half his black company dead with him
in the first assault on Fort Wagner, South Carolina.

Honors came to those who survived.
But only art could take up where history ends—
character, sacrifice, vision, courage, bravery
sculpted in the visual immediacy of living action,
vital presence. His parents rejected
a proposed free-standing equestrian statue for him:
his rank not high enough. Nor would they hear
of moving him from the grave where he had been
tossed in mockery: he would want to be
where he fell, with his fallen men.
Saint Gaudens individually modeled faces
from bearded old soldier to young drummer leading:
determined, serious figures crossing horizontally,
men marching on their souls.

Before them their leader sits on his horse.
He centers the column in deep relief. His face
is sensitively drawn, his back ramrod straight,
straight as the rifles vertically shouldered,
bristling by his side—a soldier among soldiers,
a man among men, one race of weathered bronze.

He commands an army of underground cars now.
In the stench of Boston Common
he flowers like the poppies
the flying angel above him holds
flowers of death, sleep, remembrance.

SEEDTIME AND HARVEST

But for the women—none with a name—
where would the flower and food gardens
have come from at journey's end?

She—wife of Noah—could get
no attention: he, busy hurrying
the snails along: "It's not too late";
filling the deep hold with huge
creature pairs: "No room, no room" to her.

It was the same with the wives
of Shem, Ham and Japheth, hammers
in haste against the Flood,
too noisy to hear.

Who but four women found aprons
pocket-room enough to bring on board
what the men had not provided for—
seeds and spores, bulbs needing
to be divided for more?

They hover near me in the grass—
four women without a name, yet loved,
and loving a garden as I do,
leaving a whiff of cinnamon
from the carnations they pass.

IN SUN AND SHADE

I have come to notice where the sun is
and is not, what parts of day
crimson, magenta, white impatiens
are lights for shade, and light is
yellow tulips row on row brimful of sun.
On the phone wire, in the air,
in the leaves, bird follows bird
to sing its speech.

The muck of flower beds is pleasing now.
I plant from a wheelbarrow of seeds
and nursery boxes. Clumsy still,
I feel your presence in these days
of wonder—life returning,
bee, bright flower.

Arms in oversize sleeves, I mind
the pricks less and less.
A whack across my eyes, a sliver
in the skin strangely compose me.
I bend to the work you began,
all not spoken being spoken, all
not done, getting done,

you beside me; you, my dear green thumb.

UNEQUAL EXCHANGES

No castle ramparts, no Himalayan
solitude inviting reflection,
only the back yard of a house
I've lived in since 1969,
centered in seven evergreens,
prosaically, perennially burying
themselves in their own needles
and cones, in the running light
of the variable floor, and a robin,
rubber-soled, neither too far nor
too close, pausing on ground
both ours, looking with me
into shade, narrowing his look
toward mine down to the invisible
point our sightlines make, meeting—

the local detail of pine, the soft
footwork of the floor, the deep-feeding
garden hose to the roots scrapped
in a moment of pure mandate,
a silent exchange—perhaps only
truthful comfort of the shade, perhaps
something like a shade of thought.

THE WORLD AS BEAUTY

Almost
hidden from the
road, a little canyon
to be explored. Warned of rattlers,
I bring
no stick
but burden of
perplexities, nature's
part to turn me from rock to the
valley
of love
and delight in
an apple tree's full white
blossoming, a serpent nowhere
in sight.

Photo by Robert Kendig

ABOUT THE AUTHOR

Ida Fasel is a New Englander who, with her husband, taught college courses in Connecticut, Oklahoma, Texas and eventually settled in Denver, Colorado. She earned degrees from Boston University and a Ph.D. from the University of Denver. She has been honored by Boston University with election to the Collegium of Distinguished Alumni and now holds the title of Professor Emerita from the University of Colorado at Denver (UCD). A distinguished poet, she has authored 12 volumes and 3 chapbooks of poetry. Her numerous prizes include publication awards for one book and two chapbooks, as well as two Boston University Alumni poetry prizes. Hailed as a Milton specialist, Dr. Fasel is also a first generation Star Trekkie, a balletomane, and an avid angel collector.

Milton on My Mind, is the fruit of Dr. Fasel's life-long pursuit of the meaning and music of John Milton's *Paradise Lost*. This book is definitely a labor of love, bringing together her years of teaching the works of Milton, as well as the many papers she's delivered at national and international conferences. At age 100, Dr. Fasel began compiling her essays and poems for this book, and two years later it was completed. There is no doubt that Milton has been on her mind longer than most students of Milton have been alive. It is her ardent desire that future readers of *Paradise Lost* will find this book to be a helpful and inspiring companion.